DIGGING DEEP

Exploring Me and My Health Challenges

This book belongs to

_____

My age and my health challenges

_____

This is my private journal.
Please do not read it without my permission.
Thank you for honoring my request.

RESONANCE HOUSE

RESONANCE HOUSE

Resonance House strives to help children and teens facing serious health challenges overcome the emotional burdens of their illness or disability by leading them, through journal writing, to their own inner strength.

Resonance House LLC is a wholly owned subsidiary of Silicon Valley Community Foundation. Through partnerships with children's hospitals, health organizations, and donors, Resonance House strives to make *Digging Deep* available to support every child struggling with health challenges.

Contact www.diggingdeep.org or info@diggingdeep.org to:

- Request a book for a child or teen with serious illness;
- Learn how to purchase *Digging Deep* or apply for scholarship books;
- Make a donation or sponsor books for your favorite hospital or other organization;
- Follow our blog for expert advice on meeting the emotional needs of children with health challenges.

Resonance House (USA)
1288 Columbus Ave. #255
San Francisco, CA 94133
info@diggingdeep.org
www.diggingdeep.org
(800) 488-3202

Copyright © 2014 by Rose Offner and Resonance House
First printing October, 2014
Second edition July, 2015

ISBN 978-0-9891039-1-6
Printed and bound in Hong Kong
Book design by Rose Offner: www.roseoffner.com
Cover design by Rose Offner and Neminn Win, www.winthedesigner.com

This book is dedicated to all the kids and teens with ongoing health challenges, their families, and the professionals who work with them. Thank you for helping us to understand your struggles, and for sharing your triumphs.

CONTENTS

EXPLORING
MY LIFE

HOSPITALS,
DOCTORS, AND
TREATMENTS

ANGER, FEAR, AND
UNDERSTANDING

FAMILY, FRIENDS, AND CIRCLES OF SUPPORT

LOVE AND GRATITUDE

CHALLENGES, CHANGE, AND GROWTH

YOUR JOURNEY AND HEART'S DESIRES

The Heart of the Matter

Having a serious illness is really tough and usually scary. We hope this book will make it a little easier. Everyone's experience is unique, but young people with different health issues share many of the same challenges.

You're facing difficulties that most kids your age never have to think about. Do you look or feel different from before? You may not be able to take part in your favorite activities. People might ask uncomfortable questions, tease you or, worse yet, just stare. All of this can be confusing and cause you to worry.

This journal is a private place to explore yourself: your struggles, triumphs, and dreams. Writing helps us discover who we truly are. By the time we finish journaling about a problem or question, we often find that the answer was inside of us. As we write, we're able to face our deepest fears and find the courage to overcome any obstacle.

We—Rose and Sheri—are friends and coauthors. After giving a journaling and art workshop at a conference for children with illnesses, we decided to write this book. We were touched by how kids could share their toughest feelings—inspiring everyone around them to cry, laugh, and express the truth. Both of us are passionate about helping people heal through the power of art and writing.

As a young child, Sheri had a series of eye operations, so she spent lots of time in hospitals. The volunteers thought of fun things for her to do, even though her eyes were bandaged. When Sheri turned sixteen, she became a playroom volunteer to help other kids get through their hospital visits. As a young adult, Sheri discovered that she had cancer—a brain tumor.

At first, she was terrified, because she knew just how sick the treatments had made the kids she'd helped as a volunteer. But then she remembered the spirit, positive attitude, and bravery of those children, and it inspired her. Through dealing with her own illness, Sheri learned how to dig deep and unleash her innate power to heal.

That was more than 25 years ago. Sheri is extremely grateful that her cancer has gone away, hopefully forever. Surviving cancer helped her to realize that she could do whatever she put her mind to. Today, Sheri fulfills her passion of supporting children in hospitals and medical camps. She loves to make art, play dress-up, and create journals with kids.

As a teenager, Rose found that journaling provided a safe place to explore feelings. Through the process of writing and art she was able to express her emotions, find her voice, and gain clarity. From a young age, she found that to combine images, art, and text to make beautiful hand-made journals was powerful. When she was depressed, creative writing lifted her spirits.

Rose is now a writer, artist, and instructor. Through her ongoing workshops and books, she inspires kids and adults to write, paint, and share their deepest feelings. Rose believes everyone has a story to tell, and that the power to heal is unleashed through the process of writing, and listening to each other's stories.

Exploring My Life

Self-exploration means honestly asking ourselves questions about who we are and what we're feeling. Listening to our bodies, hearts, and souls is a gift we can give ourselves—a gift

that helps us to love ourselves and realize how special we are, no matter what. Being special isn't about what you can do or what you look like, it's about who you are on the inside.

A sickness is just one small part of who you are. When you recognize the parts of yourself that always shine, especially in difficult times, you can find your way through any challenge.

Hospitals, Doctors, and Treatments

Going to doctors and hospitals is confusing; you never know what's going to happen next. Having tests or getting shots might make you feel like you're an experiment. Sometimes you may sense that people are making decisions about your life for you, without asking your opinion.

Lots of kids hate hospitals. Wearing a stupid-looking gown or using a bedpan can be embarrassing. I.V. hookups, needles, and taking medicines are unpleasant and annoying. Machines at hospitals can be frightening, too. It's often lonely and uncomfortable when you're away from home. You miss your own room, your bed, and all your stuff. Being separated from your family, friends, and school can also be depressing.

However, in the middle of all this, there can be happy surprises. Cards from classmates and gifts from visitors remind you of everyone who loves you and cares about you. While treatments and medicines sometimes make you feel worse, at least for a while, remember that doctors and nurses are working hard to help you. Still, having mixed feelings about these experiences is normal.

Anger, Fears, and Understanding

Feeling scared or angry when we struggle with an illness is natural. But it's the anger and fear we *don't* express that can get stuck inside and further depress us. Putting our feelings into words and pictures helps to soothe us.

Sometimes writing can make us feel vulnerable. You might even begin to cry as you express yourself. When we cry, we're admitting our feelings, and that takes courage. Journaling will help you tap into your inner strength—a reminder that your spirit is stronger than any illness.

Family, Friends, and Circles of Support

Family and friends bring some of life's greatest joys, but also tribulations. We find out who our true friends are when life challenges us. They call, visit, share themselves, and listen to us. Real friends encourage us to be better and stronger than we are, and they don't bring us down. They understand us even when our families can't—helping us to feel that we belong.

It's important to remember that everyone reacts to illness differently. Certain people are afraid, and don't know what to say. Sometimes when you need support the most, you may feel like you're not getting it. Other times, your relationships may grow stronger than ever, because you realize how important you are to each other. You might even meet new friends and families undergoing the same things as you are. Regardless of where you find support, being surrounded by a circle of love has great healing power.

Love and Gratitude

Sometimes when we're ill, we get annoyed easily and end up irritating and mistreating the people we love most. When we're grouchy, we can find it tough to even like ourselves. At times we might also feel guilty because of all the attention we're getting. But, if we stop and consider how those closest to us are rallying for us, we just might experience love in a way that we never have before. By reaching out and expressing our gratitude to others, we realize the perfection and power of love that comes from giving and receiving.

Challenges, Change, and Growth

Change is a natural part of growing up, but a health challenge or disability often brings about unexpected changes with difficult adjustments. There may be times when you think you can't bear it. Use your journal to unload these problems and pour all your feelings out. Once you admit that sometimes life feels like a black hole, you'll probably find there's nowhere to go but up.

Our challenges are usually our greatest teachers. Through journal writing you'll gain insights and discover tools for coping with many of life's challenges. You just may learn that you're stronger and wiser because of what you've been through.

Your Journey and Heart's Desires

Our dreams and goals are important. They help us to follow our hearts through the tough times and give us something to look forward to. Imagination and passion are vital ingredients for turning dreams into reality.

When grappling with an illness or disability, you may find yourself trying to figure out the meaning of life when nothing seems to be turning out as planned. Daring to dream lifts our spirits and empowers us. Writing and creating art helps us to make sense of our world, and leave our unique imprint on it. Use this journal to discover your dreams and heart's desires. That will be the first step toward making them happen!

How to Begin

Your journal is for you, about you, and by you. It's up to you to choose how you want to use it. There are no rules. You don't have to start at the beginning and work to the end. You can turn to a page that you feel is right for that day and start there. If you're struggling with something in particular, find a question that relates to your concerns. When we write about a problem that's bothering us, taking the time to reflect and listen, something magical happens; the answers come from within.

Feel free to write directly over the art. Your written words will make the art look even more beautiful. Don't worry about mistakes—in fact, make one on purpose and get it over with! Some of our favorite works of art came out of what at first seemed like a mistake, just as some of our most important lessons have also come from mistakes.

If you have trouble starting, or tend to ramble, ask yourself, "What am I really trying to say?" Speak from your heart, not from your head. Often this means writing quickly and not thinking too much. Some questions in the journal may be more difficult to answer than others. If one question doesn't interest you, or seems too tough, it's okay to leave it for another time. You can always come back to it when you feel ready. Courage actually comes from facing things that frighten us; and when we realize we can tackle our problems, there's often a sense of relief and satisfaction.

If you don't have the energy to write in your journal, you can ask someone else to write down what you say. Working on your journal with another person will give you a way to talk about those thoughts and feelings that might otherwise be uncomfortable to express. You may want to share what you've written with a parent, brother, sister, friend, nurse, counselor, or teacher.

There will also be thoughts, feelings, or fears you want to keep private. If you leave your journal out, someone might invade your privacy. If this happens, still, don't stop writing!

Decorating Your Journal

Your journal is a place where you can freely express all facets of your creativity. Embellish it with stickers, pockets made from construction paper, and decorated envelopes. Pockets and envelopes can be great places for private thoughts—those you don't want to share with anyone. To make a pocket, simply cut a piece of heavyweight paper in half, place one half somewhere on a journal page, and glue or tape the bottom and sides only. You can draw, paint, or collage your pockets and envelopes. Here are some ideas you might like (you can also come up with your own):

In a *garbage pocket* you can throw away the fears, doubts, and negative thoughts you write down, as well as anything someone has said or done that's hurt you. This will help you to let go of the past, your current frustrations, and everything that's bothering you.

An *anger pocket* is a safe place to put your anger and frustration. Writing on separate pieces of paper and keeping them in an anger pocket will allow you to journal without holding back, fully expressing those feelings you might not want anyone else ever to know about. This will give you the freedom to rant, rave, and get it all out. Writing about your anger on black paper with gel pens can be liberating, and looks really cool, too.

A *pocket for unsent letters* is where you can put writing that expresses your anger, hurt, or frustration. Unsent letters are those you write to particular individuals but never send, allowing you to express your pent-up feelings. You will probably notice that you feel less upset after writing them. Writing unsent letters works very well for a lot of people.

A *love pocket* holds your most cherished letters, cards, and keepsakes that you want to save. Pull out these items from your love pocket and reread them any time you need to lift your spirits.

As you fill in your journal, experiment by using gold or silver metallic pens (they leak sometimes, so be careful), colored pencils, gel pens, and glitter glue.

If you run out of writing space, simply continue on another sheet of paper, title it, and slip it into one of your pockets.

You may like creating journals so much that you'll want to continue and start a new journal from scratch. Just make pieces of art with borders, combine these pages to form a book, make up questions that inspire you and answer them, or just start writing.

So now you know the why's and how's of journal keeping. Have a good journey and enjoy the process!

Exploring My Life

My Stellar Self

We're all special. Write about your unique talents, skills, and strengths. What do you do well?

Metamorphosis

Sometimes when we get diagnosed and have to adjust to health challenges, it may be hard to remember who we really are. Describe the changes you're going through now, and how you feel about them.

Good Energy

What gives you energy and what wears you out? How can you create opportunities to enjoy the friends or activities that boost your spirits on low-energy days?

Pieces of Myself

We all have many parts. Together, they make us unique, like a one-of-a-kind puzzle. Any illness or disability is just one part of you. Describe the other aspects of yourself and the various parts of your personality.

Missing Out

When we feel we're missing out, it's a great opportunity to try something new. Write a paragraph about what you are missing out on, and then make a list of activities, hobbies, and experiences that you could enjoy.

The Masked Me

Masks are one way of hiding who we truly are. Sometimes we feel one way on the inside but act a different way on the outside. Draw the mask you are showing people and write about it. Then write about how you are really feeling on the inside.

School Daze

What are your favorite things about school? What challenges have you had to confront? What can make the difficult times easier?

If you're not in school, what do you miss about it? What do you think it will be like when you go back? What would make it easier?

Hospitals, Doctors, and Treatments

An Upside-Down World

Sometimes life isn't fair and things happen that we can't immediately understand. Have you ever wondered, "Why Me?" Describe what you felt the day you were diagnosed. What do you understand about your illness now that you couldn't back then?

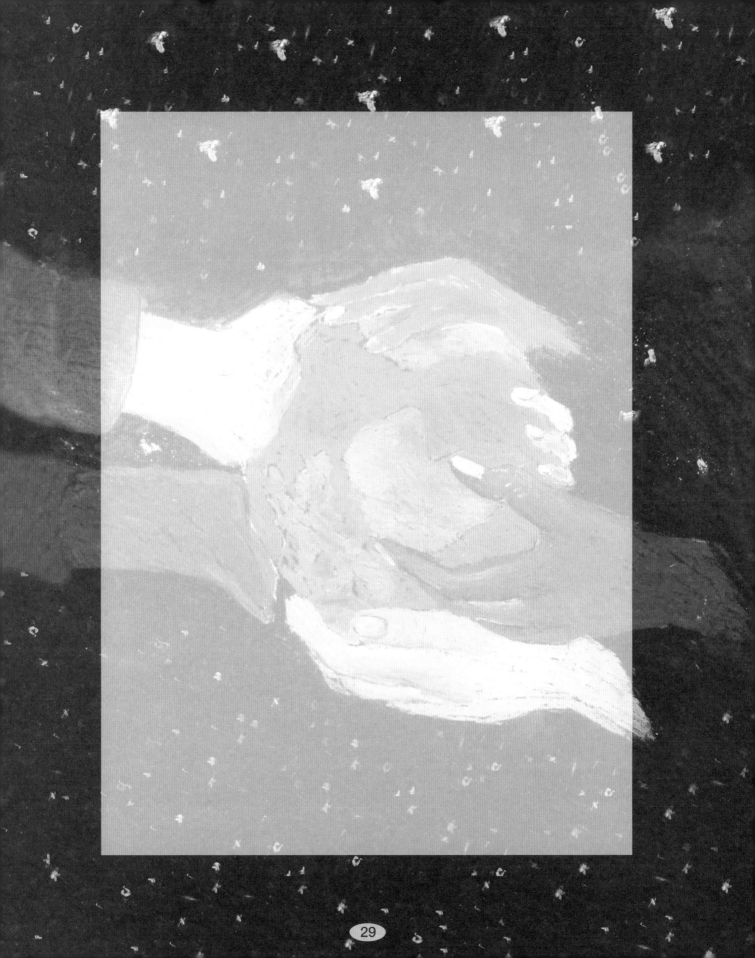

Medicine Time

If you are like many young people with health challenges, you take medicine, have treatments, or both. How do medicines and treatments make you feel? How do they affect your life?

Letter From My Younger Self

Holding a marker in the hand you don't normally use, write a letter to one or both of your parents. Begin, "Dear Mom" or "Dear Dad" or whatever names you use with your parents. See what comes out.

Home Away from Home

Hospital stays away from your family can be frightening. Some kids feel safer and more comfortable when a room feels like home. Make a list of the belongings you would like to bring with you the next time you have to stay in the hospital, at camp, or anywhere away from home.

Tricks up My Sleeve

With health challenges, it's often difficult to manage all the responsibilities and information you have to keep track of. What have you figured out or learned to make taking care of yourself easier? Are there parts of your treatment where you take charge?

Just the Opposite

Do you ever feel like you just don't want to do what the doctor says? Write about a time when you didn't follow the doctor's orders and explain what happened. Who helps you to take care of yourself?

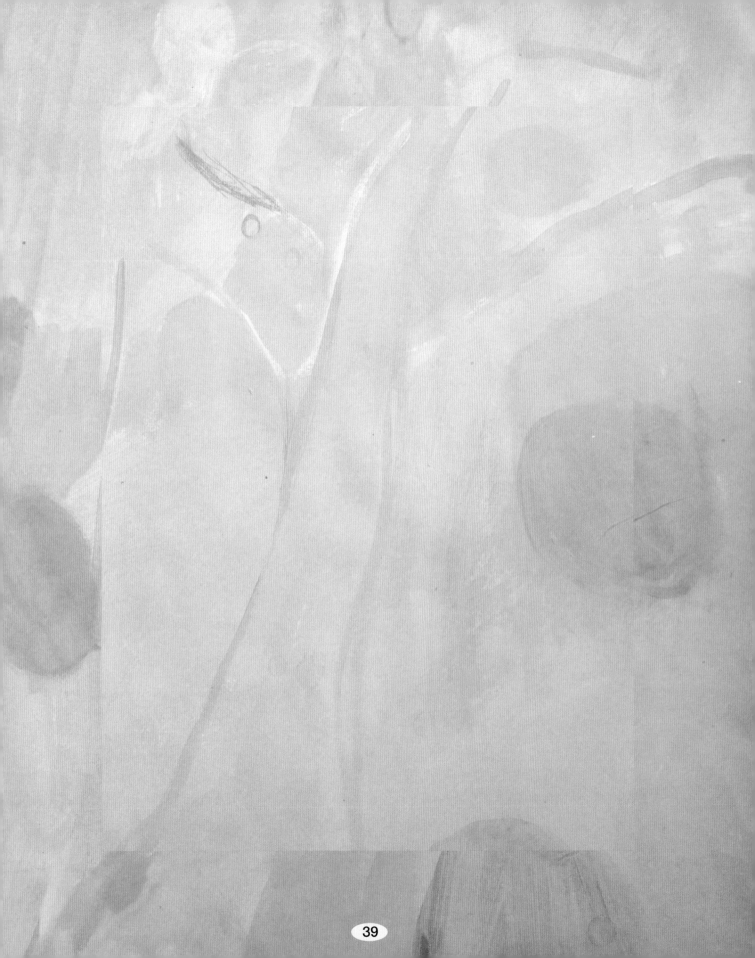

Checkups and Hospitals

When young people have to go to the doctor or hospital, they often feel anxious. That's normal. Describe how you think your medications or treatments work. Then empower yourself by making a list of questions to ask your parents, doctors, or other care providers.

Talking Too Loud

Often what people fear most is what they don't understand. Write about things you've overheard that left you feeling unsettled and worried. What do you think people are not telling you that you want to know?

Oh No, Not Again!

Getting sick again can be really heartbreaking. How are you able to rally and fight back? What have you learned that can make it easier for you this time?

ANGER, FEAR, AND UNDERSTANDING

I'm Scared

What's your greatest fear? As you describe it, imagine that each and every word you use diminishes the power of what you are afraid of. Keep going until it's all out on the page and no longer inside you.

Life Awards You

Give yourself an award that you truly deserve.

In honor and recognition of your courage, we hereby present

(Your Name)

With this award for:

Write about your award here.

Feelings

Writing is a safe way to get your emotions out. Write a paragraph or more about your three most frequently experienced feelings.

anxious aloof Energetic Shocked joyful Calm
grouchy Withdrawn stressed Alienated
peaceful Apprehensive Conflicted
awful Shy Hopeful
mi serable confident
cautious exposed mad
Loved centered creative
alienated courageous
Happy centered Regretful alone
indifferent confused Playful relieved
impatient withdrawn nervous Foolish Happy
Thoughtful Perplexed
Overwhelmed adored
tired delighted Terrified cold
frazzled Determined

The Wild Ride

A serious illness or disability has ups and downs, with many feelings happening at the same time. Describe your illness or disability as a wild ride.

A Sea of Tears

Sometimes people are afraid that if they start crying they might not be able to stop. Crying is a way of releasing pent-up emotions. When do you find yourself crying? Describe how you feel after you cry, or write about the tears you hold back.

My Boiling Point

It is normal to feel frustrated or angry when you have health challenges. Some people yell, others explode, and some become quiet and withdrawn. List situations that trigger your anger. Put those that make you furious at the top of the list and those that merely annoy you at the bottom. Use this list to keep things in perspective the next time something happens that makes you mad.

Short Circuit

Often people who are sick or in pain find that they snap at those they are closest to. Do you ever find that you have a "short fuse"? How can you express your impatience and frustration in a better way?

Difficult People

When people are grouchy, mean, or hurtful, their outrageous behavior is beyond your control. The next time you're up against a bully, choose how you will react. You could say something positive to yourself to help counter their meanness, or choose to let it go. Just don't take it personally! After trying one or more of these strategies, write about the outcome.

Lightening Up the Load

What do you do to help yourself make it through the day? Laughing, joking around, playing video games, reading a good book, or listening to music can help you relax and feel good. Describe a time when you did something to lighten the load. Make a list of the activities, experiences, or people that lift your spirits.

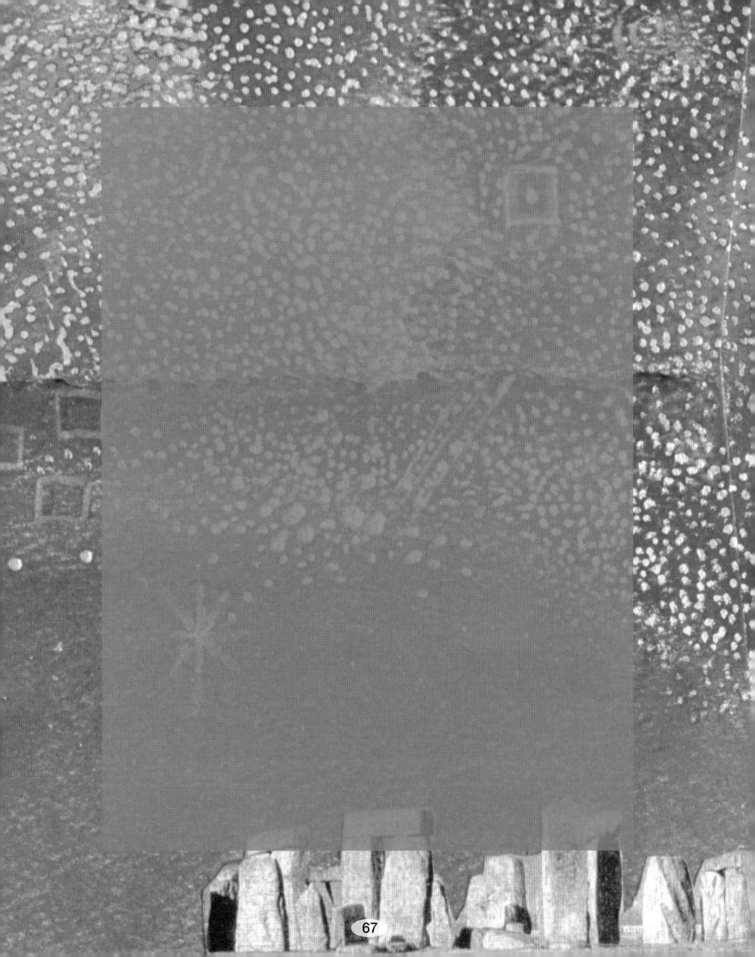

FAMILY, FRIENDS, AND AND CIRCLES OF SUPPORT

Reaching Out

Who are the people that reach out to you? What do they do or say that makes you feel cared for and supported? Write about the times when you have felt alone. In what ways have you been able to ask for help?

Family Matters

When someone in a family is sick or has a special need, the whole family is affected. How do you think your family life is the same, or different, from that of other families?

Mean Spirits

Sometimes people, even friends, can be mean. Write about an incident when someone was mean or made fun of you because you were different. Describe your reaction.

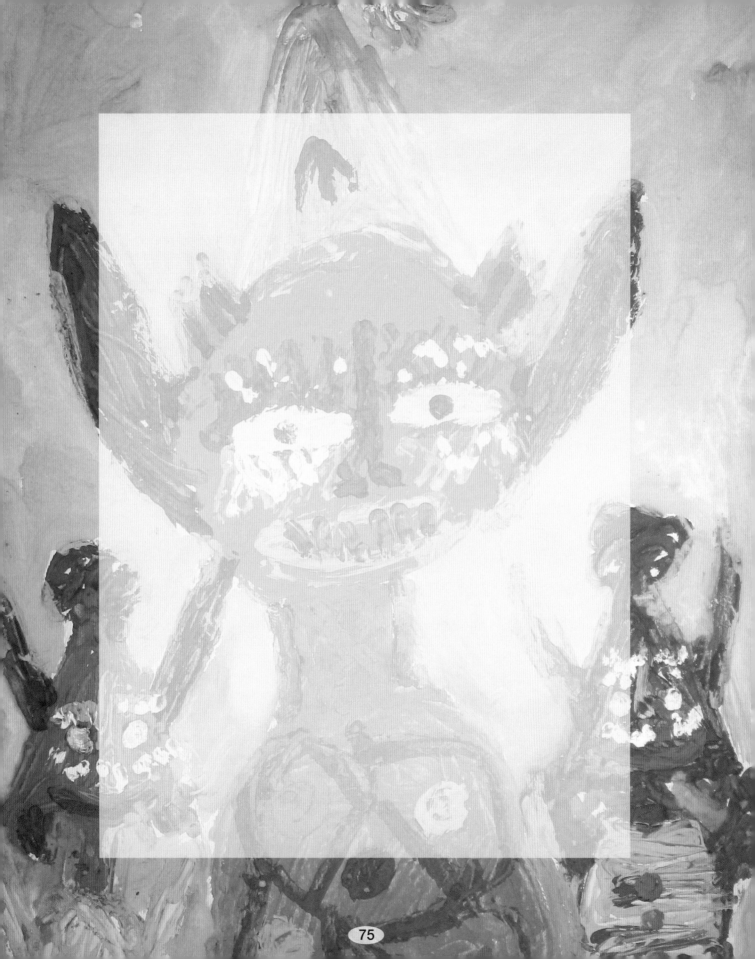

Talking, Listening, and Hearing

At times, it may seem like your family and friends just don't understand. Who can you talk to? Who doesn't hear or listen to you? Write about what you would like to tell those who are not listening so that they could understand.

Getting It All Out

It is normal to feel angry and frustrated, given all you are dealing with. Unexpressed anger can take up a lot of energy that could be used for healing. Expressing anger in healthy ways helps clear the air and will give your immune system a boost. What makes you angry? The next time you are angry or frustrated, start by writing: "I am angry/frustrated because_____."

You can create your own envelope or pocket for your private thoughts and anger, then glue it here.

Good Fortunes

Imagine that everyone on your support team wrote positive thoughts about how great you are and put them into fortune cookies for you to open. What would they say? Close your eyes and listen to what you imagine, and write what you hear in the spaces.

Center of Attention

Being the center of attention can make some kids feel great and others feel self-conscious. Describe a time when you received special attention and how you felt about it.

Unique or Different Friends

Describe your unique or different friends. What have they brought to your life?

Beginnings and Endings

Write about a friendship or family relationship that has changed or ended. Describe what happened and how it has affected you.

LOVE AND GRATITUDE

Loving Yourself

Before you can love others, you have to love yourself. What do you like or dislike about yourself? How might you feel more confident or accepting of who you are?

Heart Songs

There are so many ways to have fun. What makes your heart sing? What brings you joy, lifts your spirits, and makes you happy?

Letters of Forgiveness

Write a letter to someone who has hurt you, someone you would like to forgive but don't know how. Express any hurt or sadness in a letter you will write but not send. Often, after writing this kind of letter, we feel a sense of peace and resolution.

You can create your own envelope or pocket for your unsent letters, then glue it here.

Memory Bank

Our memories, experiences, and stories form our lives. Write about your favorite memories and why they're special. Keep an ongoing list and read it when you're feeling blue.

Words of Praise

Imagine that you have received a letter from your parents telling you that they are proud of you. Allow them to express their love and pride in this letter, that you write and receive with an open heart.

You can create your own envelope or pocket for favorite letters and cards from loved ones, then glue it here.

Acts of Love

Being told we are loved is one of the greatest gifts we can receive. Make a list of what makes you feel loved, cared about, and special.

CHALLENGES, CHANGE, AND GROWTH

Feeling Different

Everyone can feel sensitive to what others think. What are you self-conscious or embarrassed about? Are there aspects of yourself that have grown or that you appreciate more because of your illness or condition?

Attitude

An attitude is a message to others about how you're feeling inside. We all have attitudes. What has your attitude been recently?

My Armor

There are times when people feel that they need to protect themselves from something or someone. When do you put your guard up and why?

Throwing Out the Trash

Make a "garbage" pocket from a paper bag and glue it here. On separate slips of paper, write down any doubts, fears, or negative thoughts that may be interfering with your happiness. Throw them away in the garbage pocket and let these thoughts and feelings go.

Angels Fly

Imagine that you have received a message from an angel. Close your eyes, take a deep breath, and begin writing. "Dear (your name)_____"

Once upon a Time

Write a fairy tale or short story about a challenge you've overcome, the lessons you've learned, and the gifts you've received. Show how you triumphed in the end.

The Key

Young people with health challenges often refocus their priorities to reflect what's really important. What in your life is just not as important as it used to be? Where do you devote your time and energy now? What do you most appreciate in life?

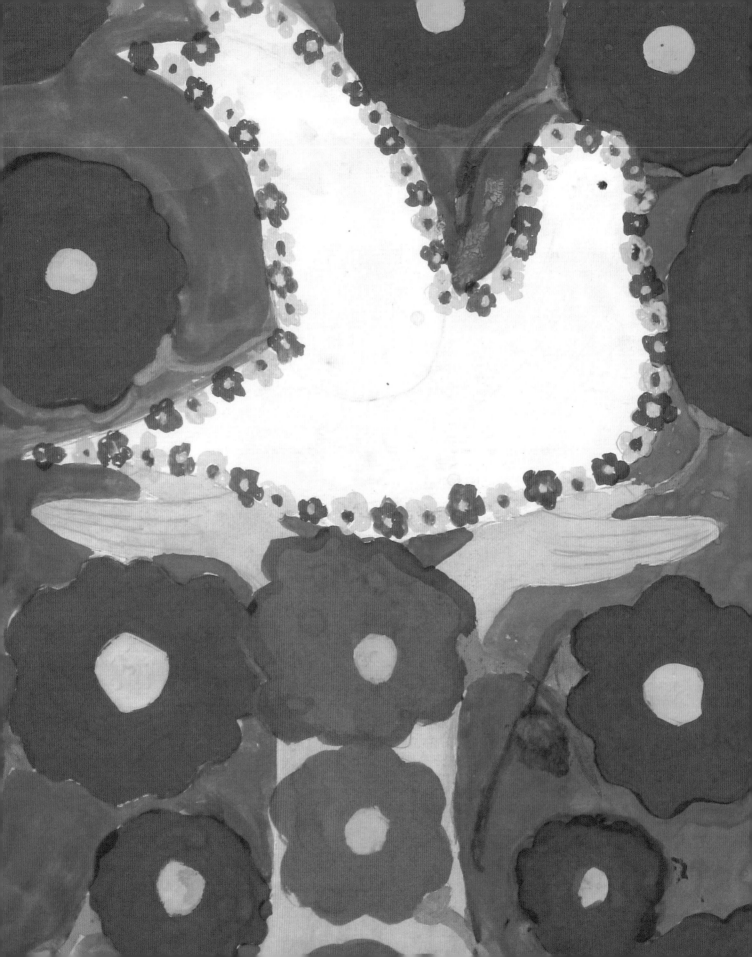

Your Journey and Heart's Desires

Blessings After a Storm

Blessings can come from difficult situations, just as a beautiful rainbow may follow a storm. When you experience challenges, see if you can find the hidden blessings and write about them here.

The Power of Peace

Peace comes from accepting your situation even though you don't like it. With illness, acceptance means you can still put up a fight, but can quit struggling over what you can't change. What are you currently grappling with and how might you find peace?

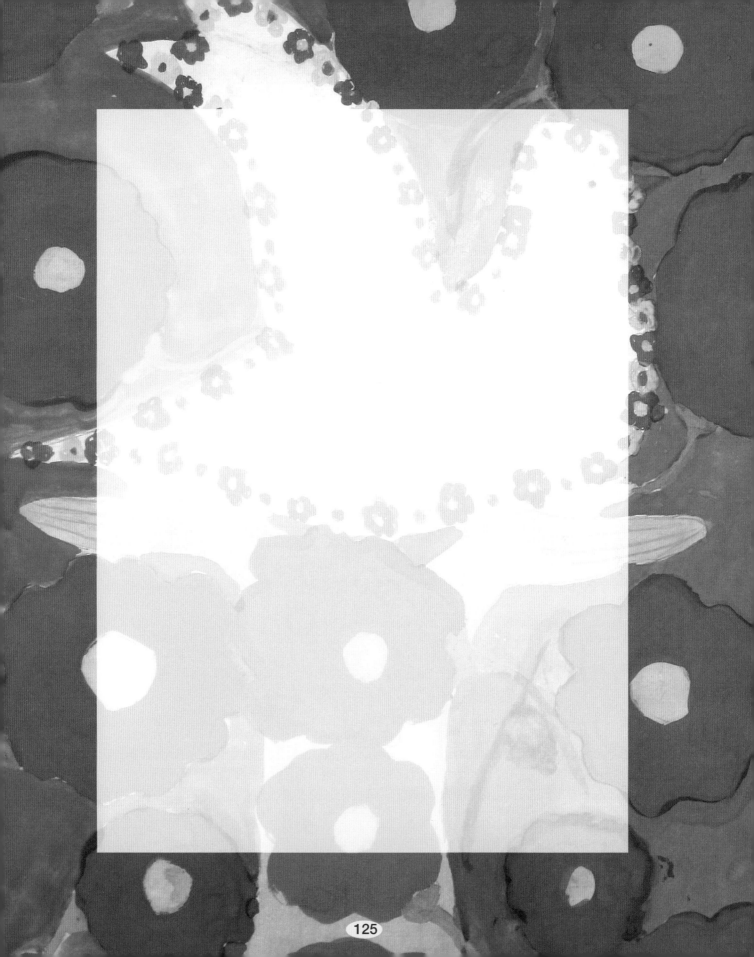

A Miracle of My Own

Our thoughts and words have power. Visualizing miracles can help to focus our energy. Close your eyes, take a deep breath, visualize your miracle, and begin writing. Then concentrate on your miracle by picturing it in your mind each day.

100 Dreams and Desires

To get what you want in life, you must know what you desire. Write a list of your heart's desires, dreams, and goals. Put a check next to each as it comes true. It is empowering to know you can create what you want in life.

1. _____ ☐
2. _____ ☐
3. _____ ☐
4. _____ ☐
5. _____ ☐
6. _____ ☐
7. _____ ☐
8. _____ ☐
9. _____ ☐
10. _____ ☐
11. _____ ☐
12. _____ ☐
13. _____ ☐
14. _____ ☐
15. _____ ☐
16. _____ ☐
17. _____ ☐
18. _____ ☐
19. _____ ☐
20. _____ ☐
21. _____ ☐
22. _____ ☐
23. _____ ☐
24. _____ ☐
25. _____ ☐
26. _____ ☐

27. _____ ☐
28. _____ ☐
29. _____ ☐
30. _____ ☐
31. _____ ☐
32. _____ ☐
33. _____ ☐
34. _____ ☐
35. _____ ☐
36. _____ ☐
37. _____ ☐
38. _____ ☐
39. _____ ☐
40. _____ ☐
41. _____ ☐
42. _____ ☐
43. _____ ☐
44. _____ ☐
45. _____ ☐
46. _____ ☐
47. _____ ☐
48. _____ ☐
49. _____ ☐
50. _____ ☐
51. _____ ☐
52. _____ ☐
53. _____ ☐
54. _____ ☐
55. _____ ☐
56. _____ ☐
57. _____ ☐
58. _____ ☐
59. _____ ☐
60. _____ ☐
61. _____ ☐
62. _____ ☐
63. _____ ☐

64. _____ ☐
65. _____ ☐
66. _____ ☐
67. _____ ☐
68. _____ ☐
69. _____ ☐
70. _____ ☐
71. _____ ☐
72. _____ ☐
73. _____ ☐
74. _____ ☐
75. _____ ☐
76. _____ ☐
77. _____ ☐
78. _____ ☐
79. _____ ☐
80. _____ ☐
81. _____ ☐
82. _____ ☐
83. _____ ☐
84. _____ ☐
85. _____ ☐
86. _____ ☐
87. _____ ☐
88. _____ ☐
89. _____ ☐
90. _____ ☐
91. _____ ☐
92. _____ ☐
93. _____ ☐
94. _____ ☐
95. _____ ☐
96. _____ ☐
97. _____ ☐
98. _____ ☐
99. _____ ☐
100. _____ ☐

Finding the Answers

You may have other questions that have been weighing on you. Write your own questions here and imagine that you know the answers.

Sharing My Wisdom

You have been through a lot and may be the wiser for it. What wisdom would you share with other young people?

More Questions

Now that you have finished this journal, you can continue to write, and make your own journal with writing and art. Here are a few questions to get you started.

Body Talk

The body is said to house the soul. Most people are uncomfortable with how they look at some time in their lives. Are there aspects of your appearance that you are self-conscious about?

Windows to the Soul

What windows are opening or closing in your life? What are you passing through, going toward, or moving away from?

True Friends

Real friends accept, appreciate, support, and encourage you. Write about a true friend and how he or she has been helpful. Describe what makes a true friend.

Heartfelt Prayers

Write your own personal prayer, asking for whatever you want or need. Write from your heart. You can say the prayer silently or aloud with others as often as you wish. Our words have power, and often prayers give us a feeling of peace.

I Believe

Write a poem or letter about your beliefs. Begin with: I believe...

Dark Night of the Soul

A "dark night of the soul" is when you temporarily lose faith. Write about a time in your life when you experienced a dark night of the soul.

Gratitude and Appreciation

A simple thank-you goes a long way. Praise and appreciation creates a momentum of loving and helpful actions. Write letters to your family and friends expressing your gratitude. Remember also to thank them verbally.

Me and My Shadow

We all have a dark side. Your "shadow" refers to the negative side that you try to hide from yourself and others. Write about your "shadow."

IF I Knew I Could

If you knew you could what would you do?

Other People's Attitudes

Some people are uncomfortable with illness or disabilities. Describe how you are treated now, and then write about how you would like to be treated differently.

My Faith

Make a list of all the things you have faith in. Sometimes recalling what we trust or believe gives us confidence in life itself.

TO PARENTS

This interactive journal was created especially for young people who struggle with health challenges and disabilities. It was designed to gently guide your child through the process of self-exploration. The expressive writing process will unfold naturally through reflection and self-inquiry. Young people are empowered when they realize that they have found the answers within. Journal writing evokes confidence and clarity.

Your child may use the journal privately, with a group, or share it with a caregiver or counselor. If you grow concerned about emotions that your child is expressing, please reach out to a caring professional—and don't forget to take care of yourself, too!

TO PROFESSIONALS

You may be familiar with the worries and concerns of children who have health challenges. If so, this book will be an easy-to-use tool when working with them. If you are a professional who hasn't yet had the chance to experience these kids' incredible spirit, then this book—with its evocative questions—will help you to guide and support the healing journey with them. Thanks for doing what you do!

Parents and professionals, we would love to hear from you. Please write to: sharing@diggingdeep.org.

TO KIDS AND TEENS

We hope you find what you need in our book and we look forward to hearing from you, too! Please download the parent release on www.diggingdeep.org and send it along with your writing and art to: sharing@diggingdeep.org.

ABOUT THE AUTHORS

Rose Offner, MFA

Rose is an award-winning author, passionate artist, and instructor. At age 16, she began keeping journals filled with art, poems, pockets, and envelopes. She has taught journaling to at-risk-teens, incarcerated youth, women, and educators. The process of self-inquiry, writing, and art continues to guide her to ask questions and listen to her voice. Rose's ongoing workshops and books will inspire you to express your unique voice, write your stories, and share your deepest emotions. For more information about workshops and speaking engagements visit: www.roseoffner.com.

Other books by Rose Offner:
Journal To The Soul
Journal To The Soul For Teenagers
Journal To Intimacy
Letters From The Soul

Sheri Brisson, MA

Sheri spent a lot of time in hospitals as a child and young adult. She needed a series of eye operations when young and, at age 24, she was diagnosed with a brain tumor. She knows first-hand what it's like to face health challenges. Through dealing with her own illnesses, Sheri learned how to dig deep and discover her inner strength and wisdom. Through the emotional healing process following her illness, she learned to connect with others in real and honest ways; that was the true gift of her illness. One of her greatest passions today is supporting kids in hospitals and medical camps. sheri@diggingdeep.org.

Acknowledgments

We appreciate our colleagues and friends who took the time and care to review *Digging Deep* and make suggestions. We are grateful to: Gretyl Clagett, Tony Towle, Christine Vaa, Mary Ellen Peterson, MA, Theresa Reilly, Sherrie Epstein, PhD, Dale Larson, PhD, Cathy Reimers, PhD, Steve Mariotti, Jan Hagan, and Barbara E. Sourkes, PhD.

We are especially thankful to our supportive families—Rose's husband, Rick Bowman, and their grandchildren Jimmy, Kody, and Katelyn, and Sheri's husband, Eric Brisson, and their children Paul and Claire—whom we love and appreciate each and every day.

The authors wish to thank the following organizations and individuals for permission to use the images on the pages listed below:

10, 14-15, 16-17, 22-23, 24-25, 26, 28-29, 36-37, 40-41, 42-45, 47, 48, 50-51, 56-57, 58-59, 64-65, 68, 70-71, 72-73, 74-75, 76-77, 82-83, 84-85, 86-87, 92-93, 102, 104-105, 106-107, 112-113, 114-117, 120, 124-125, 126-127, 128—licensed children's art;

12-13, 18-19, 20-21, 30-31, 32-33, 38-39, 46-47, 52-53, 54-55, 60-61, 62-63, 66-67, 78-79, 80-81, 88, 90-91, 94-95, 96-97, 98-99, 100-101, 108-109, 110-111, 118-119, 122-123, 129-131, 132-133, 134-135, 136-137, 138-139—licensed from Rose Offner;

7, 34-35—licensed from Char Pribuss.

Kraash Font used with permission.